W9-BCU-309

Riches of the Earth

**Irene Franck and David Brownstone**

GROLIER

An imprint of Scholastic Library Publishing
Danbury, Connecticut

## Credits and Acknowledgments

*abbreviations: t (top), b (bottom), l (left), r (right), c (center)*

Image credits: Agricultural Research Service Library: 1b (Michael Thompson); 3, 6, 13l, and 26 (Scott Bauer); 4; 5, 11, and 22r (Keith Weller); 17 and 20 (Brian Prechtel), 19 (Jack Dykinga), 22l (Peggy Greb); Art Resource: 16 (Gilles Mermet); Getty Images/PhotoDisc: 7r (C Squared Studios), 12 (Mitch Hrdlicka), 13r (John A. Rizzo); Getty Images/PhotoDisc/PhotoLink: 7l (S. Solum), 8r-9 (C. Borland), 14 (D. Falconer), 23 (J. Luke); Kansas Wheat Commission: 8l; National Aeronautics and Space Administration (NASA): 1t and running heads; North Wind Pictures: 27; Photo Researchers, Inc.: 10 and 29l (Rosenfeld Images/Science Photo Library), 15 (Holt Studios International/Bob Gibbons), 28 (Holt Studios International/Nigel Cattlin); U.S. Department of Agriculture: 21 (Tim McCabe), 29r (Ken Hammond); Woodfin Camp & Associates: 24l (Jonathan Blair), 24r-25l and 25r (Marc and Evelyne Bernheim). Original image drawn for this book by K & P Publishing Services: 18.

Our thanks to Joe Hollander, Phil Friedman, and Laurie McCurley at Scholastic Library Publishing; to photo researchers Susan Hormuth, Robin Sand, and Robert Melcak; to copy editor Michael Burke; and to the librarians throughout the northeastern library network, in particular to the staff of the Chappaqua Library—director Mark Hasskarl; the expert reference staff, including Martha Alcott, Michele J. Capozzella, Maryanne Eaton, Catherine Paulsen, Jane Peyraud, Paula Peyraud, and Carolyn Reznick; and the circulation staff, headed by Barbara Le Sauvage—for fulfilling our wide-ranging research needs.

Published 2003 by Grolier
Division of Scholastic Library Publishing
Old Sherman Turnpike
Danbury, Connecticut 06816

For information address the publisher:
Scholastic Library Publishing, Grolier Division
Old Sherman Turnpike, Danbury, Connecticut 06816

© 2003 Irene M. Franck and David M. Brownstone

All rights reserved. Except for use in a review, no part of this book may be reproduced, stored in a retrieval system, or transmitted in any form, or by any means, electronic or mechanical, including photocopying, recording, or otherwise, without prior permission of Scholastic Library Publishing.

Library of Congress Cataloging-in-Publication Data

Franck, Irene M.
Wheat / Irene Franck and David Brownstone.
p. cm. -- (Riches of the earth ; v. 15)
Summary: Provides information about wheat and its importance in everyday life.
Includes bibliographical references and index.
ISBN 0-7172-5730-4 (set : alk. paper) -- ISBN 0-7172-5727-4 (vol. 15 : alk paper)
1. Wheat--Juvenile literature [1. Wheat.] I. Brownstone, David M. II. Title.

SB191.W5F74 2003
633.1'1--dc21

2003044091

Printed in the United States of America

Designed by K & P Publishing Services

# Contents

**Fields of ripening wheat, like this one being harvested in the American heartland, call to mind the "amber waves of grain" from the popular song "America the Beautiful."**

# Amber Waves of Grain

The "amber waves of grain" in the early lines of the song "America, the Beautiful" are very real to anyone growing up in wheat-growing country. In the United States that might mean almost anywhere, from the Atlantic to the Pacific and from Canada to the Gulf of Mexico. It especially means the big wheat-growing "breadbasket" states of the Midwest and Northwest.

In the wider world those amber waves of grain stretch a long way farther. Huge quantities of wheat are grown every year by many of the world's peoples, as has been true for thousands of years. People growing up in China, Russia, Canada, India, Argentina, France, and many other countries see fields of wheat reaching out to the horizon, just as Americans do.

Wheat has long been one of humanity's most basic and important foods. This began to be so in Egypt and the Middle East more than 10,000 years ago. That was when people began to plant, farm, and harvest wheat, becoming some of humanity's earliest farmers. Before then people had only gathered wild wheat for food, rather than growing it. As farming spread, wheat spread with it, becoming one of the staple foods of the ancient world.

Today there are thousands of varieties of wheat and foods made from wheat. These foods include many kinds of breads, rolls, biscuits, waffles, pastries, muffins, doughnuts, pie crusts, cookies, cakes, breakfast cereals, spaghetti, macaroni, noodles, couscous, and much more. There are hundreds and perhaps thousands of special wheat foods in scores of countries, and their names are in many languages.

**Seeds from ripened wheat (like the stalks in the vase at the upper left) are ground into flour to make all of these varied and delicious products, including breakfast cereals, pastas (the colored shapes in the bowl at center right), and breads, cakes, cookies, rolls, and other baked goods of all kinds.**

Today we know that wheat is a major source of greatly needed proteins, vitamins, minerals, fiber, and energy-supplying carbohydrates (see p. 10). As our grain mills make flour, they also add many substances that enrich wheat foods, in the process preventing many diseases (see p. 29).

By far the greatest amount of wheat produced is used in human food. Some wheat, however, is used as animal feed. Wheat has also been used in several industrial products, among them ethyl alcohol, starch, and several kinds of glues.

Wheat contains many kinds of nutrients (nourishing substances; see p. 10). That is why wheat in the form of flour has also provided highly prized emergency help for hundreds of millions of people in times of famine, epidemic disease, and war.

In our time wheat is humanity's greatest food, feeding billions of us all over the world. Much more wheat will be needed in the years ahead, for the world's population continues to grow tremendously fast. There are more than 6 billion people on the planet Earth in the early years of the 21st century. Within the next 50 years—and that is within the lifetimes of most of us now reading this page—there are likely to be twice that many, or 12 billion.

**Wheat is used in all sorts of foods, including breakfast cereals like that in this tempting spoonful with milk and strawberries.**

The kernels (seeds) are the parts of the wheat that we eat. These develop along spikes that grow from the wheat plant, as on this one. This is an "ear" of wheat, as a corn cob is an ear of corn.

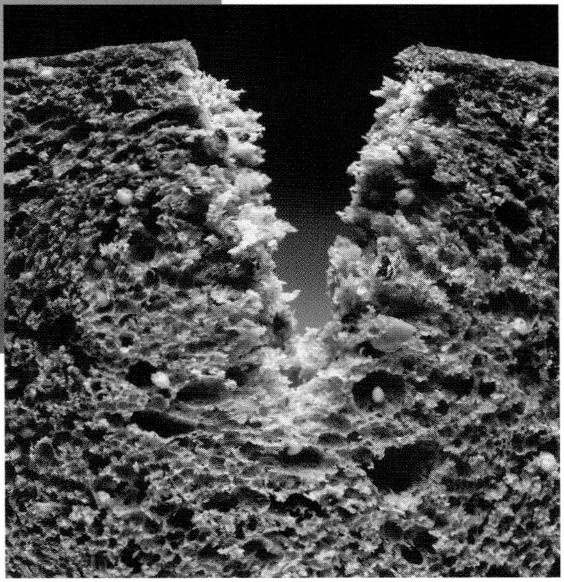

Gluten in wheat stretches when flour is made into dough, letting air into the dough. You can see the air pockets in this slice of bread being torn in half. However, some people are not able to digest gluten, so they cannot eat foods made from wheat.

# What Is Wheat?

The edible part of the wheat plant—the part we eat—is the *kernel* (seed), a cereal grain that is a small piece of the wheat plant. The wheat plant is a member of the grass family, as are barley, rice, rye, oats, and corn (maize). All together, these are the main cereal grains that have been feeding humanity for thousands of years.

The wheat plant is a tall, green grass. Fully grown, it is usually between 24 inches and 48 inches high, though some varieties of wheat may be a good deal taller. (All varieties of wheat belong to a group of cereal grasses that biologists call *Triticum*.) Modern wheat growers prefer shorter plants, called *dwarf varieties*. That is because the edible part of wheat is the kernel, rather than the rest of the plant.

Each wheat plant grows from a single kernel. The body of the wheat

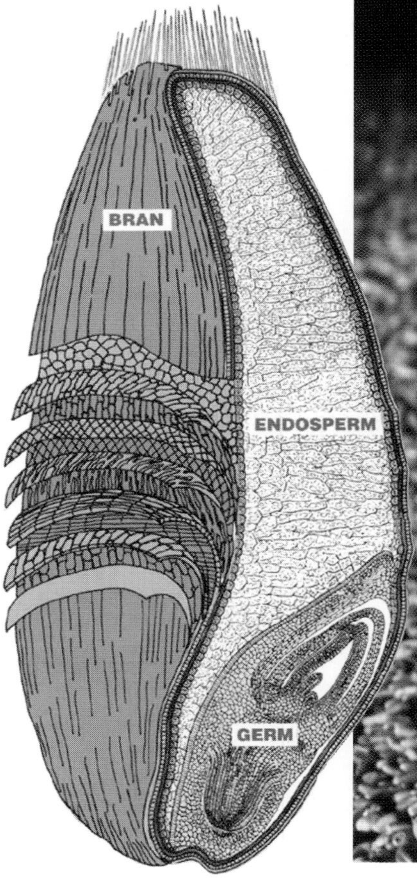

**This drawing is a cutaway view of a single kernel of wheat. The bran is various layers making up the brown outer covering. Inside it are the endosperm (the white matter) and the germ, from which a new wheat plant can grow.**

plant is made up of roots, stem, the leaves that sprout from the stem, and the many stalks of flowers, called *spikes*. The spikes are where the wheat kernels develop. Each spike can carry as many as 50 tiny kernels.

As the wheat plant grows, it uses water and nutrients drawn in through its roots. Its green leaves also use sunlight, carbon dioxide (a common gas) from the air, and water to make various carbohydrates (see p. 10), in a process called *photosynthesis*. These are the wheat plant's main source of energy.

Late in the growing season the wheat plants dry out. When that happens, their color turns from green to gold. Then they become the

This is what wheat grains look like after they have been harvested and separated from the rest of the plant but before they have been ground up into flour.

"golden fields of waving wheat" that have caught people's imagination for thousands of years.

## Wheat Kernels

Each kernel of wheat has three parts. The protective outer cover of the kernel, made of up of many thin layers, is called its *bran*. Inside the kernel is a very small portion called its *germ*. In a very real sense, this is a seed within a seed. That is because, when a kernel of wheat is planted, the new wheat plant actually grows from the germ. The third part of the kernel is the *endosperm*. This makes up more than 95 percent of the inside of the kernel. The endosperm contains the substances used as food either by the growing new plant or by humans.

Some wheat kernels are set aside to be used as seeds for new wheat plants. However, most wheat kernels are harvested and ground into flour, becoming food for humanity. Wheat is generally cooked to make it tastier and easier for our bodies to digest (break apart to get the nutrients).

The basic process is simple: We grow the wheat, harvest its kernels, grind up the kernels into flour, and use that flour to make bread and many other foods. The process has been followed for thousands of years and continues to happen today, even though today we use large, complex machines to help us do it.

For making bread, the flour is mixed with water (or some other liquid) and often some seasonings, shaped into a loaf, and baked. Usually something such as yeast is added to make the bread "rise"—that is, to build up some gases to make the bread lighter and airier. The result is called *leavened bread*. Without such additions the bread is called *unleavened* or *flat*, such as pita bread.

## Wheat for Health

Wheat kernels are made of just a few main substances. Most of the kernel—almost 70 percent—is made up of *carbohydrates*. These are chemical compounds (mixed materials) composed of the elements (basic substances) carbon, hydrogen, and oxygen. Carbohydrates are part of the cells of every living thing and are necessary to human life. They come in many different forms. The carbohydrates in a wheat kernel are about 60 percent starch, with smaller amounts of *cellulose* (fiber) and several types of sugars. Starch and the sugars found in wheat are major sources of energy, while fiber is essential to the health of the human digestive system.

Wheat kernels also contain *proteins*. These, too, are basic chemical compounds necessary to human life. All proteins contain the elements carbon, hydrogen, oxygen,

**This baker is pouring the ingredients for bread into a kneading machine, which mixes the materials (primarily flour, water, seasonings, and often yeast) into a dough. After kneading, the dough is shaped into loaves like those at the right and then baked.**

**Wheat comes in many different kinds and varieties. This scientist is examining some short, stubby clubhead wheat grown in the Pacific Northwest.**

and nitrogen, while some also contain other elements. Proteins are largely made of special substances called *amino acids*. Human bodies cannot make all the different kinds of amino acids they need to stay alive. To get some of them, humans must eat plant proteins. The proteins in wheat are very good sources of many amino acids, as well as energy.

Wheat is also a good source of several other substances important to health. Among them are several vitamins and minerals, including vitamins E, $B_1$, $B_2$, and niacin, and the minerals calcium, iron, and phosphorus. Wheat products are often enriched with other vitamins and minerals to make them even more nutritious.

## New Varieties of Wheat

Farmers and plant scientists have long bred wheat to keep desired qualities and create new ones. For most of human history that has meant selecting disease-resistant seeds of the highest possible quality for planting the next year's crop of wheat.

During the 20th century knowledge of the science behind plant breeding grew. Then wheat breeders focused on crossbreeding wheat varieties to produce healthier, higher quality and wholly new varieties of wheat far faster and more surely than ever before.

Starting in the mid-20th century, the development of new varieties of wheat and several other grains enabled crop production to rise sharply, especially in many of the world's poorest and least developed countries. The resulting much higher and healthier crop yields were so good that the whole set of improvements came to be called the *Green Revolution*.

In the late 1900s scientists also began to make changes in the wheat plant's genes, the basic biological codes that guide its growth and development. This *genetic engineering* has developed new and attractive varieties of wheat. However, it has also raised concerns that altering a plant's genetic codes might damage people and the environment. The long-term effects of such genetic changes are still unknown.

## Kinds of Wheat

Several main kinds of wheat are grown around the world, and within those main kinds there are thousands of varieties. The most basic differences among varieties have to do with whether the kernels of wheat in each kind are *hard* or *soft*, mainly *red* or mainly *white*, and planted in *winter* or *spring*.

Whether wheats are hard or soft depends on how they are meant to be used. Hard wheats, which are high in proteins, are especially high in *gluten*. This is a kind of protein that stretches and lets air into dough as it is made out of flour, making bread light and airy. Because of this, the hard red winter, hard red spring, and hard white wheats are all used mainly in bread and rolls. The hard white varieties are also used for noodles.

Another kind of hard wheat is *durum wheat*. This is used to make pasta products, including spaghetti and macaroni. The gluten in durum

**Wheat is a very nutritious food. This "food pyramid" shows the kinds of foods we should eat every day. The largest amount (shown at the bottom) is food made from grains such as wheat.**

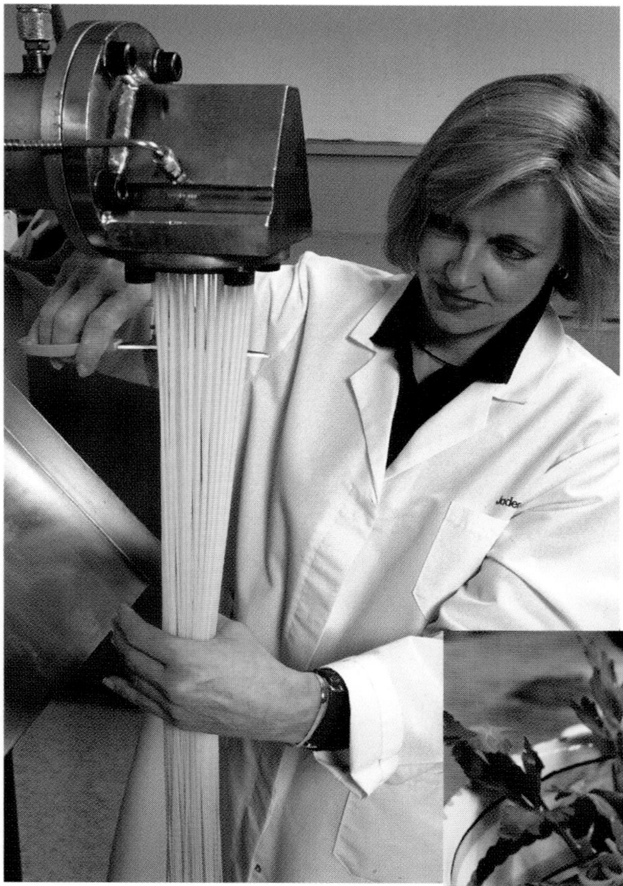

Durum wheat, one of the kinds of hard wheat, is used to make pastas of all kinds. This food technician is making spaghetti by hand in a laboratory to compare the quality of the pasta made from different varieties of durum wheat.

Wheat is at the heart of many of our favorite foods, including pastas like spaghetti (made of durum wheat) shown here in a dish with shrimp, tomatoes, and various seasonings.

wheat is the key reason that pasta products do not stick to each other when cooking, though other substances are also used to cut stickiness.

The soft red and white wheats are used for cakes, crackers, some kinds of breads, pie crusts, and many other bakery products.

Whether wheat is planted in the winter or spring depends largely on the climate. In the United States, for example, farmers generally plant winter wheat in the fall. It grows until freezing winter weather comes, lies dormant (inactive) in the ground in winter, and then grows again until it is harvested in the spring. Spring wheat is planted in early spring and grows until it is harvested in the fall.

**From "breadbasket" regions such as central North America and large sections of Eurasia, wheat is transported throughout the world. Here it is being transferred from a huge grain elevator (at right) onto a cargo ship.**

# Wheat around the World

Great advances have been made in wheat breeding and in the varieties of wheat now grown throughout the world. Even so, wheat still grows best in cool to cold, dry areas with warm to hot summers, and with growing seasons long enough for either spring wheat or winter wheat. Adequate water is necessary for wheat, but the main varieties of wheat do well in a dry climate, rather than a very humid one. Because of these needs for dry, cool conditions, most of the world's wheat is grown in a massive band of north temperate zone countries that stretches from the Rocky Mountain chain across North America and Europe all the way out into Central Asia.

The greatest of all of the world's "breadbasket" areas is the Great Plains of North America. This is a huge region that includes much of the American Midwest and West, along with Canada's "prairie provinces" of Manitoba, Saskatchewan, and Alberta.

A second great "breadbasket" area includes much of central Russia west of the Ural Mountains and also Ukraine. This has long been one of the world's major wheat-producing regions.

A third substantial wheat-growing region lies on the plains of northern China. Western Europe, including much of Germany, France, Italy, and several other countries, also produces a good deal of wheat. Large quantities of wheat are also grown in India, Australia, and on the plains of Argentina. Smaller amounts are grown in many other countries.

## Early Wheat Farming

The history of wheat is a story of change and development over thousands of years. Much evidence indicates that the kind of wild wheat called *einkorn* was being gathered and used as food in some parts of the Middle East as long as 14,000 to 16,000 years ago. That was thousands of years before farming was invented, largely in the same areas.

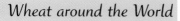

**Thousands of years before farming was developed, people gathered and ate a wild variety of wheat called *einkorn*. This is some ripe einkorn wheat from modern Britain.**

Wheat has been an important food for many thousands of years. The Roman goddess of agriculture, Ceres (who gave us the word *cereal*), is shown here gathering wheat. Dating from the 200s, the picture—a *mosaic* formed from small colored pieces—comes from a home in Tunisia in northern Africa.

No one yet knows exactly when farming became widespread. However, it is clear that wheat was being farmed in ancient Egypt, what is now Iraq, and several other regions in southwest Asia by at least 8,000 years ago, and probably 10,000 to 12,000 years ago. The two main early varieties of wheat were *einkorn* and *emmer*. Most modern varieties of wheat were developed from them. Of the two, emmer became by far the main kind of wheat farmed in the ancient world. Barley was probably farmed a little before wheat, but wheat was the first major cereal crop.

Early farmers, like farmers ever since, planted wheat kernels as seeds. Then they tended the wheat plants as they grew and harvested the wheat when it was ready, holding some seeds for planting in the following year.

## Spread of Wheat Farming

By 6000 B.C. wheat was also being raised in southern Europe and by 2000 B.C. in northern Europe all the way to Britain and Scandinavia. In this later period wheat was also being grown to the east in Iran and India.

Wheat farming first reached the Americas from Europe in the late

1400s. That was when Spanish invaders, explorers, traders, and settlers brought it to the Caribbean and Central America.

In the early 1600s wheat was also introduced to North America, in French-held Acadia (now Nova Scotia), Virginia, and New England. Wheat farming then started to spread across North America, as European immigrants began to force Native Americans out of their homelands, providing vast new farmlands for the new settlers. In later centuries wheat cultivation spread widely in the Americas.

Wheat cultivation also spread around the world. From the 1600s it reached the western Pacific, the South Pacific, and Africa.

## Wheat and Hunger

As part of the Green Revolution (see p. 11), work continues to improve the quality and quantity of the world's wheat (and other cereal grains). Despite this, world hunger is a huge and growing problem. Billions of people throughout the world are hungry every day of their lives, and hundreds of millions are always in danger of famine.

There are many reasons for this. One is that populations continue to grow very fast in most of the world. Another major reason is that many countries and their people are so poor that they cannot afford to buy the food they need to survive.

Yet there is no great shortage of wheat and other major foods in the

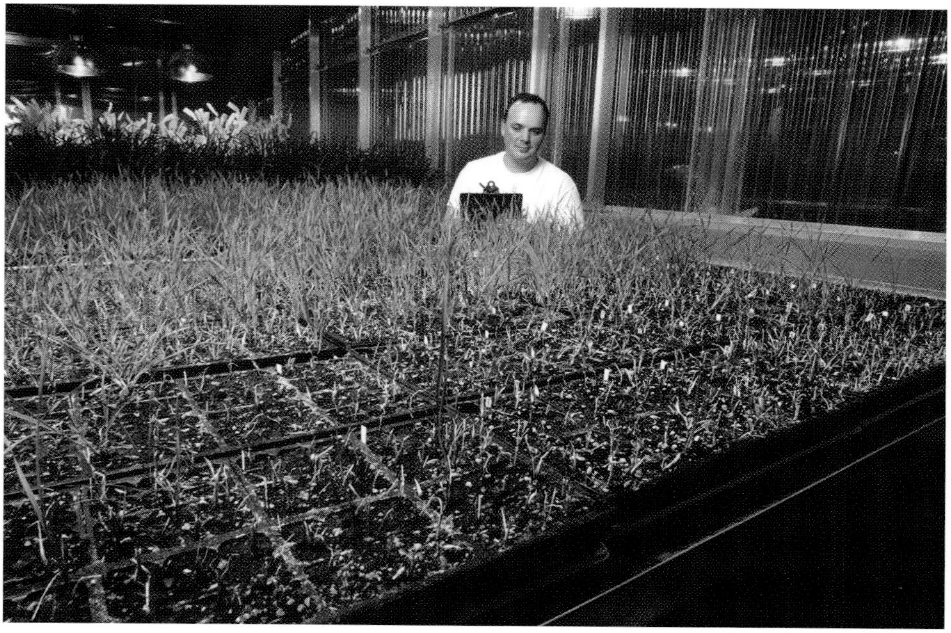

**Scientists are working to improve different varieties of wheat so they can be grown in many more places. This scientist is examining how well young wheat plants survive freezing temperatures.**

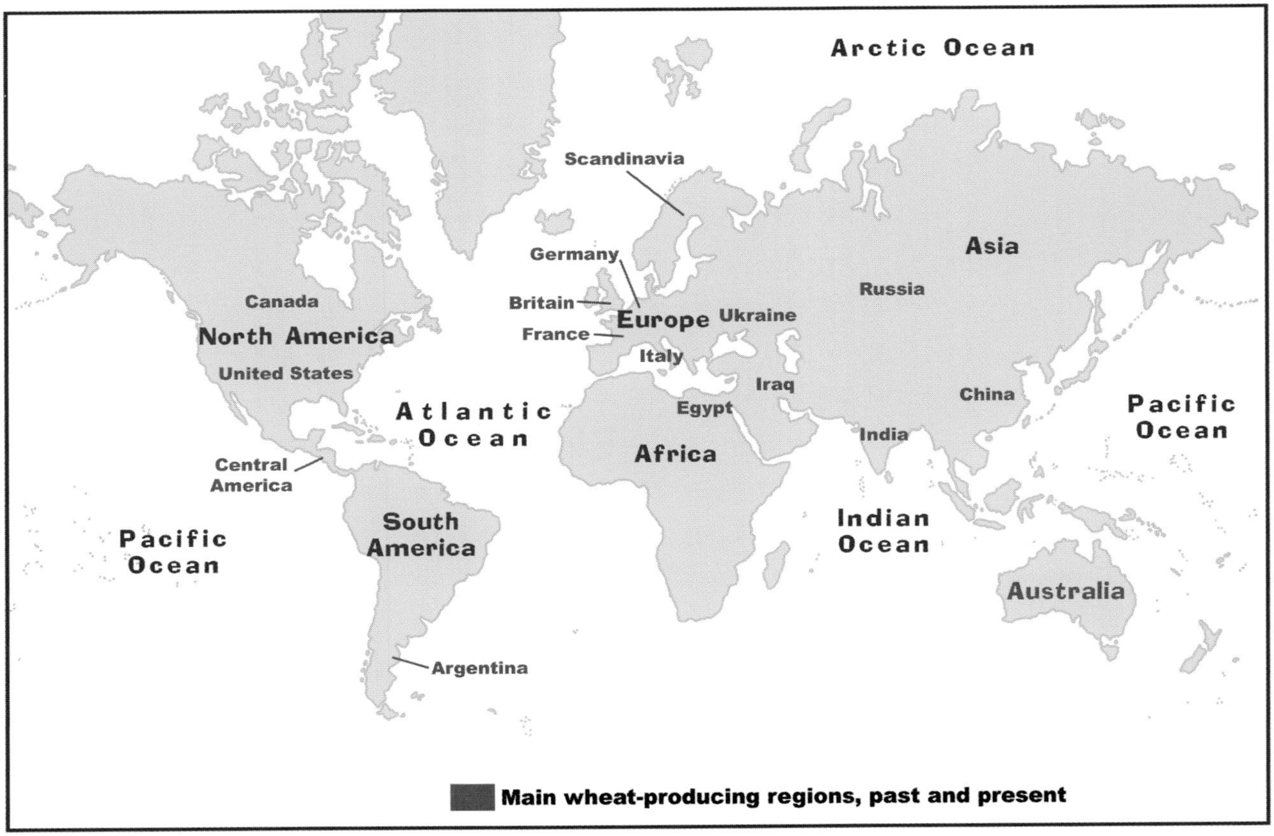


world. The world's farmers routinely produce considerably more wheat than is eaten, and they are capable of producing much more. During many years very large farm surpluses, including wheat, are stored by the United States and several other governments.

Sometimes the stored surplus is used in years when crop yields are low. Some of the surplus is also distributed in the form of disaster relief. Sometimes the surplus is never distributed at all, or is used as farm animal feed. What is missing is the money to buy the wheat.

How to solve such huge and growing problems as worldwide hunger and poverty is one of the most important and urgent questions facing humanity. It has so far proven far from easy to resolve—which makes it no less important and urgent.

These scientists are examining special wheat in a field. The wheat variety is special because it has been grown to resist a fungus that often damages or kills normal wheat plants.

# Planting and Growing Wheat

Growing wheat is very different today from what it was in earlier times. Today most of the world's wheat is seeded, cultivated, and harvested with the help of powerful machines. In earlier times this work was done by large numbers of farmers and farm workers.

Yet the basic processes themselves have not changed, all the way from planting to harvesting. As was done thousands of years ago, wheat seeds are still put into the plowed ground (*sown*) to grow into wheat plants. These produce edible kernels of wheat and are harvested, with the kernels and the plants themselves bound for several kinds of uses.

When to plant, how much seed is

When the wheat plant is young it is green, like most grasses. Working in a greenhouse laboratory, this scientist is examining wheat plants that have been specially engineered to be more nutritious.

used, and how deep to put the seeds into the ground vary. Today, as earlier, these depend on such factors as climate, the quality of the soil, and the varieties of wheat planted. For example, the amount of seed used in sowing an acre of land can vary widely, generally from 15 to 150 pounds per acre, but sometimes even more or less than that. How deep to set the seed into the ground also varies widely, from one-half inch to four inches deep.

What is different today is how it is all done. For thousands of years wheat was planted with the help of only a few hand tools. In earliest times these included some kind of hoe to break up the ground before seeding and to smooth it down after seeding.

Later the hoe was replaced by the plow and harrow. The plow cut long, straight furrows (narrow trenches) into the field for the seeds. The harrow was used to cover the seeds with earth, to protect them and give them a chance to grow into plants.

Still later the plow became a hand-powered or animal-powered tool. This cut a furrow, dropped seeds into it, and covered the furrow with the earth just dug out it, all in one operation.

Plows such as these are still used

in many parts of the world. However, most modern wheat farmers plant with the *seed drill*. This tool cuts furrows, measures and deposits seeds, and then covers the furrows—all in one carefully controlled operation. Many modern seed drills also drop fertilizers (substances to enrich soil) into the furrows, to help the seeds grow into plants. Seeds planted by seed drills are often so close together that the individual wheat plants can hardly be seen.

Once sown, wheat fields must be kept as clear as possible of weeds (other unwanted plants). Also the soil between the furrows must be turned over, broken up, and exposed to air (*aerated*) to help the wheat plants grow. The machines used to do this are *cultivators*. They cut weeds and turn the earth over again and again, as the wheat plants grow, mature, and approach harvest time.

## Pesticides

In many countries chemicals of several kinds are used to kill both weeds and the insects that attack wheat and other plants. Often these chemicals, called *pesticides*, are applied as spray, either from machines on the ground or from low-flying airplanes.

**Pesticides are used to try to keep wheat from being damaged by insects or diseases. Often they are sprayed by a low-flying airplane called a crop duster, like the one shown here.**

Pesticides are widely used throughout the world. Some have proven very useful in increasing crop yields, destroying unwanted plants, and fighting disease-carrying insects. At the same time, some pesticides have proved to be extremely toxic (poisonous), to people, plants, air, water, and other parts of the natural world.

By the early 21st century many early kinds of pesticides had been banned in the United States and many other countries. The most notable example of this was the pesticide DDT (dichloro-diphenyl-trichloroethane), a highly toxic pesticide that was banned in the United States in 1972. Until it was banned, it was by far the most widely used pesticide in the world. Even with its dangers, DDT is still used in many countries, as are many other banned chemicals.

This wheat kernel has been damaged by insects that feed inside the wheat grain. If many kernels are damaged, the wheat is less valuable to humans for food.

In a healthy, young wheat plant, the leaves are green, like those on the left here. However, if the plant is diseased, the leaves often turn yellow, like those at the right. The unhealthy plant can no longer grow properly.

**This is a familiar scene at harvest time in many parts of the world: a large machine rolls through wheat fields harvesting the ripe wheat and kicking up a great cloud of dust in the process.**

# Harvesting Wheat

As with planting and growing, the basic process of harvesting wheat is much the same as it has been for thousands of years. When the wheat is ready to be harvested, it is *reaped*—that is, the plants are cut off at the stem.

Next comes *threshing* the wheat. This is the several-step process of separating the all-important wheat kernels from the rest of the plant. During threshing the plant is broken up into its several parts, including the kernels, the *straw* (the stems and leaves), and the *chaff* (the head of the plant and other leftover bits and pieces). Then the kernels are separated from the rest by a process called *winnowing*. This involves tossing the pieces into the air to separate the heavier wheat kernels from the other lighter plant parts.

In earlier times these processes were done by large numbers of farmers and farmworkers. They carried out the steps one by one, at first with the simplest of hand tools and later with many increasingly com-

**In some parts of the world wheat is still harvested by hand, as here in Pakistan, using simple tools such as knives, scythes, or sickles. It is then tied in sheaves and left to dry.**

plicated labor-saving tools. All of the early kinds of tools and methods used in harvesting are still in use somewhere in the world. However, most wheat harvesting today is a highly mechanized process. It is carried out by large machines run by a few skilled people and combining many tasks into a single harvesting process.

In early times reaping was done with a simple cutting tool called a *sickle*. A larger version of the sickle is the *scythe*. The basic tool used to break up the cut wheat plant was the *flail*, a tool with a handle plus a free-swinging stick. The broken-up plant was raked, to separate the kernels of wheat from the straw and chaff. It was then thrown into the air to let the wind carry away the remaining straw and chaff, leaving the kernels of wheat behind. Threshing was later done by having people or animals stamp on the wheat to break it up. Later still the reaped wheat was broken up using heavy weights, such as rollers.

During the early 1800s, as world industry moved into the age of machines, *reapers* and *threshers* were developed. The most important of these was the horse-drawn reaper. After a series of improvements, it

As has been done for centuries, this wheat farmer in India (above) is threshing his wheat by riding over it with a heavy roller, to separate the kernels from the rest of the plant. After that is done, the pieces are tossed in the air (right) to separate the heavier kernels from the lighter unwanted parts.

could reap wheat plants, gather them, and tie them into bundles (*sheaves*) ready to be threshed. Threshing machines developed side by side with reapers.

Today most worldwide wheat harvesting uses the *combine*. This machine does all of the harvesting processes in a single operation. The combine reaps the wheat plants in the field, separates (winnows) the plants into their several parts, threshes the kernels out of the heads of the cut plants, cleans the threshed kernels, and deposits the cleaned kernels into bags or tanks for storing and further processing.

After harvesting, some wheat

may be stored in a storage bin on the farm where it was grown. Other harvested wheat may be stored in a nearby *grain elevator*, a tall storage building that can store more wheat than a home farm can. Wheat to be sold is usually moved into large grain elevators, where it is stored until it is shipped to grain mills in the United States or abroad.

However it is stored, the harvested wheat must be cleaned carefully once again before going into storage, to avoid spoilage from weather conditions, disease, and insects. It must also be carefully checked for the amount of water it is carrying. If it contains too much water, it must be dried out somewhat to avoid spoilage. Then it is ready to go on to a mill.

**The combine not only cuts the ripened wheat plant and breaks it up into parts, but also separates out the all-important wheat kernels. Those are pouring out of a chute into a truck, which will carry the grains to where they will be stored.**

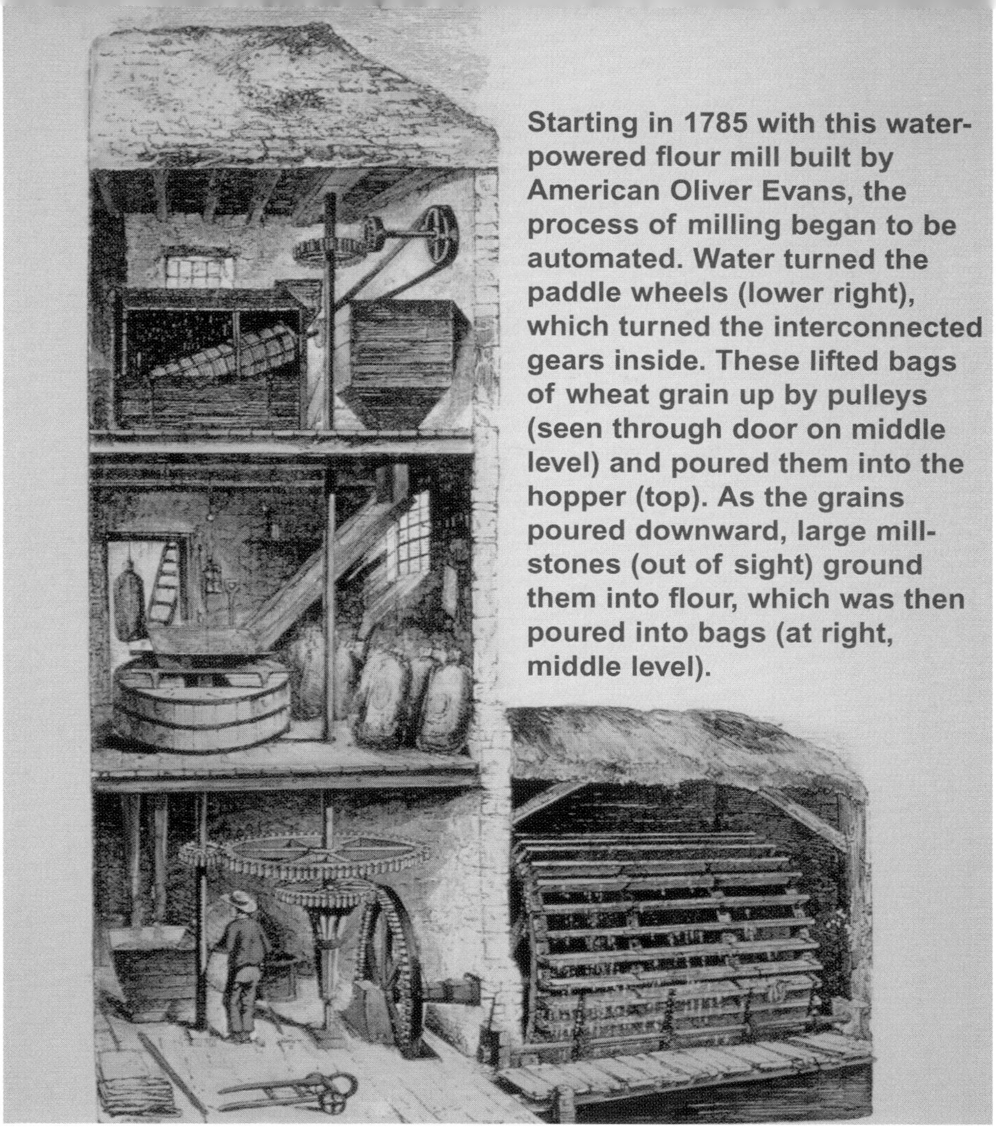

**Starting in 1785 with this water-powered flour mill built by American Oliver Evans, the process of milling began to be automated. Water turned the paddle wheels (lower right), which turned the interconnected gears inside. These lifted bags of wheat grain up by pulleys (seen through door on middle level) and poured them into the hopper (top). As the grains poured downward, large mill-stones (out of sight) ground them into flour, which was then poured into bags (at right, middle level).**

# Milling Wheat

Ten thousand years ago wheat was ground by hand. Today wheat is usually ground in a modern, high-powered grain mill full of big, complicated machines and computers. Either way, the aim of milling wheat remains the same: It is to separate the wheat kernels into their three basic parts—the endosperm (most of the kernel), the wheat germ, and the bran (the kernel's outer covering; see p. 8).

Over thousands of years the art and science of milling made tremendous advances, as new inventions and power sources came along. The great early invention, made many thousands of years ago, was the

Today in most part of the world wheat is milled entirely by electrically powered machines, most much larger than this one in Britain.

process of grinding the wheat between two heavy millstones turning against each other.

The power to turn the stones came at first from people and animals, later from water power and windmills, and still later from gasoline engines and other modern power sources. In the early 1800s the millstones themselves were generally replaced by sets of metal rollers. They, too, are run in our time by modern power sources.

In the modern mill wheat is made into several kinds of flour. These later become many kinds of bread and other foods made of wheat.

The first step in milling is to clean the wheat kernels very thoroughly. That means moving the kernels through several machines, all intended to remove anything that is not part of the kernels. The first two machines are *separators*. One uses magnetism to remove any iron or steel particles that might have found their way into the wheat. The other shakes out such leftover bits and pieces of foreign matter as straw, pieces of chaff, and very small pieces of twigs or other matter picked up in the wheat fields. Yet another separator removes any remaining small stones. Still another picks up and removes any remaining pieces of anything that does not have the same shape as the wheat kernels. A final cleaning machine rubs away (*scours*) and blows away any material that is still attached to the kernels.

Then the now-clean wheat kernels are ready for separation into their parts: endosperm, bran, and wheat germ (see p. 8). This is done by grinding the kernels down into finer and finer particles. A long series of grinding and sifting steps produce, in the end, many different kinds of flours. The endosperm is used to make white bread flour and much of whole wheat flour. The bran and wheat germ are very important for making whole wheat flour, and they also have their own special uses, as when they are used to feed animals.

Many kinds of flours are whitened (*bleached*) during milling, such as flours intended for making cakes, cookies, and other baked goods. Many white bread and bakery flours are also enriched—that is, substances are added late in the milling process to make the flour more nutritious or better-tasting. Enrichment is particularly important with white flours. That is because much extremely valuable nourishment is removed from white bread flours when the bran and wheat germ are removed during milling.

**This is a production line in a modern bakery. Workers (left) supervise the machine mixing of flour and other ingredients. The resulting dough is shaped into loaves and placed on conveyor belts, which move them to ovens for baking. At the end loaves of bread and other products are packaged for sale to customers, as here (below) on racks in a wholesale club in Virginia.**

# Words to Know

**amino acids:** See PROTEINS.
**bran** Protective outer covering of the wheat KERNEL.
**carbohydrates** Chemical compounds (mixed materials) found in living cells and necessary to human life. In wheat KERNELS the carbohydrates include STARCH, CELLULOSE (fiber), and several sugars.
**cellulose** A CARBOHYDRATE found in the wheat KERNEL. Also called *fiber*.
**combine** A farm machine that performs all of the wheat harvesting processes in a single operation, including reaping (see REAPER), WINNOWING, and THRESHING.
**durum wheat** A kind of hard wheat used mainly in making spaghetti, macaroni, and other pasta products.
**edible** Able to be eaten.
**einkorn wheat** A kind of wheat that grew wild and was gathered and eaten in the ancient world.
**emmer wheat** A kind of wheat that was widely grown by farmers in the ancient world.
**endosperm** The main part of the KERNEL; it supplies health-giving substances (nutrients) for the growing plant and food for people.
**enriching** Adding substances, such as vitamins and minerals, to improve the quality of a food; for wheat, done late in the MILLING process.
**fiber:** See CELLULOSE.
**flat bread:** See LEAVENED BREAD.
**furrow** A long straight cut made in a farm field before SOWING.
**genetic engineering** Making changes in *genes*, the basic set of biological codes that guide a plant's growth and development, to create better varieties.
**germ** The very small part of the wheat KERNEL from which a new wheat plant can grow.
**gluten** A kind of PROTEIN that stretches and lets air into dough as it is made out of flour, making bread and other wheat products light and airy.
**grain elevator** A large grain storage building.
**Green Revolution** The development of many new varieties of edible plants and farming methods that greatly increased food crop yields in many of the world's poorest countries, starting in the mid-20th century.
**harrow** To separate and smooth over the earth in a field after SOWING. Also the tool used to do this.
**kernel** The grain that is the seed of the wheat plant.
**leavened bread** Bread treated, as by the addition of *yeast*, to create gases in the dough, making it lighter and airier. Breads not treated this way are called *unleavened* or *flat*.
**milling** Grinding, as between millstones or rollers. Wheat kernels are ground into flour and other wheat products. This also involves separating the KERNELS into the BRAN, GERM, and ENDOSPERM.
**millstones:** See MILLING.
**pesticides** Chemicals used to kill weeds and insects that attack wheat and other plants.
**photosynthesis** A process by which plants make CARBOHYDRATES from sunlight, carbon dioxide, and water.
**plow** To cut long straight FURROWS into a farm field to prepare for SOWING seeds. Also the tool used to cut the furrows.
**proteins** Basic chemical compounds (mixed substances), including special *amino acids*, that are necessary to human life.
**reaper** A farming tool used to cut and harvest growing plants. The term describes a whole range of tools, from the early *sickle* and *scythe* to complicated, high-powered modern machines.
**scythe:** See REAPER.
**seed drill** A farming tool that cuts FURROWS, measures and deposits the seeds in the furrows, and covers them with earth.
**sickle:** See REAPER.
**sowing** The process of planting wheat seeds.
**spikes** The many stalks of flowers that are part of the wheat plant. The KERNELS of wheat grow from the spikes.
**spring wheat** Wheat that is planted in spring for harvesting in the autumn.
**starch** A kind of energy source that is part of the CARBOHYDRATE found in the wheat KERNEL.
**thresh** To separate the wheat KERNELS from the harvested wheat plant.
**unleavened:** See LEAVENED BREAD.
**winnow** To separate the kernel from the rest of the broken-up plant, often by tossing in the air.
**winter wheat** Wheat that is planted in fall for harvesting in the spring.
**yeast:** See LEAVENED BREAD.

# On the Internet

The Internet has many interesting sites about wheat. The site addresses often change, so the best way to find current addresses is to go to a search site, such as www.yahoo.com. Type in a word or phrase, such as "wheat."

As this book was being written, websites about wheat included:

**http://www.wheatfoods.org/**
Wheat Foods Council Grains Nutrition Information Center, offering nutritional, historical, and other information, plus recipes, downloadable images, and links to other sites.

**http://www.wheatmania.com/allaboutwheat.html**
All About Wheat, a Kansas-oriented website offering facts and diagrams about growing and processing wheat.

**http://www.kswheat.com/**
Kansas Wheat Commission site, offering facts, news, educational materials, and more.

**http://www.cimmyt.cgiar.org/**
International Maize and Wheat Improvement Center website, describing work being done to improve wheat.

# In Print

Your local library system will have various books on wheat. The following is just a sampling of them.

Baker, H. G. *Plants and Civilization*. Belmont, CA: Wadsworth, 1978.

Fenton, Carroll Lane, and Herminie B. Kitchen. *The Plants We Live On*. New York: John Day, 1971.

Franck, Irene M., and David M. Brownstone. *The Green Encyclopedia*. New York: Prentice Hall, 1992.

*From Wheat to Flour*. Sharon P. Davis, ed. Washington, DC: Millers' National Federation, 1996.

Heiser, Charles B. *Seed to Civilization*. San Francisco: W. H. Freeman, 1971.

Hinshaw, Dorothy Patent. *Wheat*. New York: Dodd, Mead, 1987.

Inglett, George I. *Wheat: Production and Utilization*. Westport, CT: AVI Publishing, 1974.

Peterson, R. F. *Wheat*. New York: Interscience, 1965.

Roberts, Jonathan. *The Origins of Fruits and Vegetables*. New York: Rizzoli, 2001.

Selsam, Millicent E. *The Plants We Eat*. New York: Morrow, 1981.

*Van Nostrand's Scientific Encyclopedia*, 8th ed., 2 vols. Douglas M. Considine and Glenn D. Considine, eds. New York: Van Nostrand Reinhold, 1995.

Vaughan, J. G., and C. A. Geissler. *The New Oxford Book of Plants*. New York: Oxford, 1997.

# Index